D0415746

Peter Campbell is a mental health system survivor. He was born and raised in Scotland and has been living in London since 1973. He was a founder member of Survivors Speak Out and Survivors' Poetry. He is a freelance trainer and writer in the mental health field and also worked for many years with pre-school children. He lives in Cricklewood, North West London and supports Hendon FC.

Brown Linoleum
Green Lawns

Brown Linoleum
Green Lawns

PETER CAMPBELL

Hearing Eye

Published by Hearing Eye

Hearing Eye
Box 1, 99 Torriano Avenue
London NW5 2RX, UK
email: books@hearingeye.org
www.hearingeye.org

Poems © Peter Campbell 2006
ISBN: 1-905082-04-5

Acknowledgements
Some of these poems have been previously published as follows:
That Pleasure in "sweet, sour and serious" (Survivors' Press Scotland);
The Mental Marching Band and *Not to Die* in "Under The Asylum Tree"
(Survivors' Press); *Crisis Advocate* in "Something Inside So Strong" (Mental
Health Foundation); *Fourth Station, Health Act* and *The Pain of Love* in
"Camden Voices 1978–90" (Katabasis); *Drugtime Cowboy Joe* and
In Your Warm Arms in "from dark to light" (Survivors' Press);
Night and Morning in "In the Company of Poets" (Hearing Eye).

To Willie Emslie won the Martha Robinson Poetry Competition, 2002.

Cover photograph by Martin Parker, based on an idea by Peter Campbell.

This publication has been made possible with
the financial support of Arts Council England

Printed and bound by Cambridge University Press
Designed by Martin Parker at www.silbercow.co.uk

Contents

That Pleasure

There is a pleasure madmen know
After the bath,
As they stand in the arms of their belt-less clothes
And the scrutineers have left the room
With a practised laugh.
There is that pleasure then.

There is a pleasure madmen know
After dusk,
As they search for gods in the pewter skies
And the scrutineer lays down Jane Eyre
Beside his desk.
There is that pleasure then.

There is a pleasure madmen know
Of their kind,
As they embrace at the pot-room door
And the scrutiny of the caring crowd has gone blind.
There is that pleasure then.

There is a pleasure madmen know
Without the wine,
That blood and reason hang themselves
On the same line
And the scrutineers dispense love
For the last time.
There is that pleasure then.

(There is a pleasure sure
In being mad, which none but madmen know! — John Dryden)

The Mental Marching Band

You'd better wet your whistles
For the Mental Marching Band
For we're making a wee comeback
And it's spreading through the land.
And we'd laugh you to distraction
If we thought you'd understand
About the Mental Marching Band.

There's Danny Ogenkenyu
On the bagpipes by the way.
And when he's took his Lithium
Sweet Jesus can he play.
You can denigrate the madness
The song won't fade away
From the Mental Marching Band.

We'll all be out and running
When the storm breaks.
Down the House of Commons
Wi' our fruitcake.
You'll have to take your medicine then
Just for the music's sake
And the Mental Marching Band.

We'll not be taking prisoners
Under blood red skies.
We've had too much confinement
In our own lives.

We're getting our own World War out
That everyone survives.
Thanks to the Mental Marching Band.
Let's hear it.

Dark Water

The water in the lade is dark as vinegar
Caddis-fly cases hold to the concrete banks
We finger them up
A small felony
Not blistering the wheel of nature.

Out nettle, in dock.
Dock shall have a new smock
But nettle shall have nothing.

The water is dark over the weir
Sheep's wool hanks cling to the wire
Spread on the table
Like old men's hair
In an empty room
Someone is there.

Out nettle, in dock.
Dock shall have a new smock
But nettle shall have nothing.

The fish lay on the damp shingle
The gullet slit
Dark water eddied around the tail
Cold as I remember it.

I held it there like a broken wrist
I hid it in the sphagnum moss.
The spokes of the wheel
Are never lost
The lapwings cry
Bewitched, Bewitched.

Out nettle, in dock.
Dock shall have a new smock
But nettle shall have nothing.

Song

Would the foxes bark if I lied to you?
Would the seagulls rise up from the plough?
If I lied and said I loved you,
Would the seasons break in two?

The mountains stand to the north of the strath,
The washlands lie down to the sea.
Would they betray me if I called you back
And made you sleep with me?

There is no sandbank wide enough,
No trout that swims so deep
As to hide the coin of a union
You never meant to keep.

The gos does not stoop in folly,
Nor the tawny owl retract.
No more can I use a sweetened tongue
To persuade you to come back.

I may choose the strings of an ancient harp,
I may place the words in line.
I am the player of the harp
But the music is not mine.

Drainage

They dug a leat through Blackhill Moss
Turves bend and seep
The haunches of the mountain lie at dusk
More vividly by such a tutored cut.

Bog boys tumble home
Plover rise from purgatory
The sky is scabbing grey
We sit at Gulabin reading into the night.

Midday the turves are soft
Peaty and fuming from the warm land
The drain crawls with ants.

We pick among the broken roots
We turn the flat stones up
The earth is juicy
Sweet and black.

The curlews stop in Mob's Field
We wipe our hands with grass
Swinging back to the house with our pouches full.

In the cold white kitchen
Beside grouse feet and pickled adder
We separate the bodies out for preservation.

Clipping the blue labels
Writing in copperplate
Arthropods from the moor
Summer nineteen eighty-three.

Inside The Garden

In a Surrey asylum garden
There are peonies, large and showy.
There is *Quercus robur* shading the hollows.
Butterflies, colours founded in Eden.
But there are no smiling natives.

They swarm in behind the doors,
Lagged to their ears with tobacco smoke and peace-cake.
Tinkling us for favours,
Shanked up like ricketty ponies
Out of sight of the fairground.
Yellow, mournful, dull.

Laughter dies here
A maiden run to mud.

The food comes from a central place in cylinders,
Hustled between the lawns in unapproachable convoys,
Arriving smashed and waxy.
They hover in porches, hungry before the bell.

The horticultural detail plant onions
In the old walled orchard.
Squat among tomato frames sharing boiled sweets.
Seventy-five per cent non-productive,
Holding the barrow and rake,
They tip their heads to nurses
In brief colonial tribute.

We have farmed here with care
Not wilderness nor oasis.

A green and pleasant fourteen acre wood.
A cricket pitch
With magpies feeding and a clubhouse
For the membership. A little England
For ruling of the mad.
An exhibition for the sane and unbelieving –

They have sat beneath the banks of rhododendron
With their fly-buttons undone.
They have brought out knitting,
Unravelling themselves backwards in sight
Of the flagpole.
How fine the paths are in Maytime.
How red the bricks from Bagshot.

Unease is wrapped up here
In a plain manilla.

We look in.
We polish our shoes as if for a long journey.
We pop in and out with presents from home.
There is always a clock, a nameplate
By a dry fountain.
A definition for the garden
That does not rattle in the autumn wind.

Behind the rituals of rocking at the corner,
Saying aye-aye and grimacing,

There is no mystery, no savage discourse
Of a different palate. Our nobility
Is of no other order, our brains and jaws the same,
Excepting separation and dominion make it so.

We have planted here with care
A shady empire for our nicer affectation.

Inside an asylum garden,
There are Surrey names posted on gable-ends.
There are Surrey notables in busted profile.
But this is not Surrey, this is not noble,
And there are no smiling natives.

Decisions

I tell him I am Zeop the Centurion.
He writes it down into my case notes.
In the green room he plays with paper clips,
Talks to the girl from the Migraine Unit
Decides he will sleep on it.

Next morning the staff team convenes.
Porcelain cups for psychiatrists
Plastic for everyone else.
Decisions have to be reached.
I sit on a straight backed chair.
"We don't think that you are Zeop the Centurion"
He says.
"I know that" I say.
"Why else do you think I'm in here?"

Inner View

We sat in a room with three textbooks,
Three beige walls
And a large poster for
Tranquillon the drug.

He had broad sensible fingers
That he re-arranged towards me
Across the desk, across
The desk-top edge.
Surreptitiously closing,
He was warm.
Like a salesman is warm.

Schizophrenia is a disease in the brain.
A crumbling of the bonds of personality.

We dealt from my house:
Puberty, fantasy
And heterosexual peer relationships.

He had fine hazel eyes
That caressed his catch of notes.
Addressing me across one shoulder,
He spoke like only words held meaning.

Schizophrenia is a disordered perception.
The merging of subject and object.

We pinned my childhood out in distances:
Close to, alienated from,

Fixations.
The minstrel must have lied.

He had good hands
That grasped like a civilian's
In the corridor when we came upon each other.
He had good hands
For re-assembling how I think
Of myself in the cold.
(And he wasn't asked)

He led a scientific exploration.
I stood on little peaks waving flags –
It seemed the truthful thing to do.

He had the measured eye
Of a good listener.
Of one whose certainty is never touched
(In deference to the client)
He had the measured gaze
Of Cyclops in a store of worlds.

Schizophrenia is a disfiguring of values.
To cry without cause is madness.

He played the magic twist:
Man, Microbe, Machine.
Valuing reason,
I was subverted by his self-belief.

Schizophrenia is a disease in the brain
Breaking the bounds of ego.

Devil Of The Flowers

The devil stepped out in the couthy dawn
And he kissed the baby twice.
Once for her sins on Judgement Day.
Once for her civil rights.

He walks the streets of Kentish Town
His pleasure for to seek.
He has a Jew's harp in his bag
And a snowdrop in his shirt.

He makes a pitch on Leighton Road.
He plays the Jew's harp jig.
The school comes out to drink him in,
A spug sings from the bridge.

A handsome traveller walks close by
And damns him for his song.
– By twelve o'clock you'll beg for beer
  Outside the Arlington.

The devil feels him at the wrist
And his look is awful keen.
–You took me once to Highgate Fields.
  You did not spurn me then.

–You had me down by Highgate Ponds,
  You gave me quite a bundle.
He takes a violet from his poke.
– Have one of these to handle.

– Have raspberry, have scabious.
  Have lilac and bog myrtle.
  You once denied me dignities
  To which I am entitled.

– Long, long the wintertime,
  Harsh, harsh the rain.
  I'll take the razzle out your step
  If you pass me wrong again.

– Bare, bare the mountain-side,
  Cold, cold the sea
  Each time you play my children false,
  You do a slight to me.

The devil walks in Kentish Town
His kinsfolk for to teach.
He has a brier in his hair,
Rose water on his feet.

Snowdrop – hope
Violet – faithfulness
Raspberry – remorse

Scabious – unfortunate love
Lilac – humility
Myrtle – love

The False Knight
(Reworking of a ballad)

There was a rich man on the road
To see his real estate.
And he came on a snotty wee boy
With his fish supper on a plate.

— Who lives in that house over back
And pays so little rent?
— My dad lives there, the boy replied.
His money I've just spent.

— And whereabouts his caring woman
Who lets you roam the night?
— She's in your factory baking bread.
That woman is his wife.

— You speak your answers handsomely.
You would make a handsome son.
Take some silver change off me
For the magic of your tongue.

— I will take no money for my speech
I have only answered plain.
Each time a rich man gives of his purse,
Each time he marks a name.

—Then sit with me and speak of life
For I am great in years.
— But I am young and being poor
Have even as many fears.

—Wee boy I had such shape as yours
In my young and former days.
—That you have never shared my heart
Your present shape betrays.

—You slander me with small wild words.
I never wished you ill.
—You asked me of my father's wife
And the payment of a bill.

— And you to be a rich man.
The false knight parting cried.
— And you to be a dead one,
Said the boy and still he stood.

(The False Knight Upon The Road — The Penguin Book of Ballads. 1975)

Smile, Please

The man with a camera up one leg
Is visiting Chichele Road again.

Scourge of the racketeers,
Baring his ankle at handsome Albanians,
Bosnians, Croats, tight Afghans.

Helps them into the vans.
A nod to the ganger.
Pretends he knows a hoist
From a grab.

Looks like one to let the daylight in.

Thinks that he's quite the magic eye
Who will winkle them out,
No-one suspecting,
Onto the nation's screens.

He slips in at Sheila's
Looking for promising stuff.

We're all Celts
This side of the counter.
Finds that our banter
Of waiting on pavements
In a different age,
In a whiter season

Is not what his audience need to consider.

His shirt's too sharp.
His Kilburn Times too folded.

What he wants is phrases with dots.
Something that sits well
In subtitles.
A coded look, a moody wall.

If he can get it all
In North West Two,
That would be a good result.

He's been undercover too long,
Filming on the people's behalf.

A few real days at Extraman
Might help his trim.
An early morning breath
Of grass clippings
Down Roundwood Park

Would give his lungs reasons
To be careful.

All that tackle
Down his left trouser
Cannot be good for a man
With his concerns on public display.

A wee guest spot on the 189,
Departing Brent Cross,
Might moderate his global sensitivities.

Tying Up Baby

His hands
Tying up baby
Brush on the cheekbones carefully
His chin dips into the hairline
And holds the child.

Her palms
Flatten the shoe-straps
Her thumbs
Moving the anklets
Dizzy the skin like docken stalks.

They stand by a fountain
Waiting for the upwards staircase
Fingering the karri-chair
They gaze like wolves.

Crisis Advocate

They all smiled
But the drapes were down
Thirteen nutters seen this morning
Even the constitutional niceties
Sometimes wear thin.

She did not smile
Sat next to me
Erect
In black
With Doc Martens boots on.

"We would get on much better, doctor,
If you didn't keep interrupting him".

There was a pause
The shifting of spines

A page in my history
Turning irreversibly
Forwards.

This Corridor

This corridor is green,
Green flecked with white
That we can step around
And catches
At the yellowness of light.

This corridor,
So coldly long,
Cackles with footsteps
Once each noon.
Our long stored feet ring down
Like flagrant children's
Early out of school.

A dandy staff nurse guards
By the canteen.
With his commercial smile
And casual lean,
He used to sell ice cream.
An ice cream man with a conscience.

This is no path to cadge tobacco on.
This road to Ward Supplies or Trebizond.
No call from us
Can redefine the span
Of our world picture.

Here's dust that's much too thin
To fall into the begging game.
You only win yourself a name
For being indigent
Among the bright executives
From District Management.

Do not stop here
To drum the walls
With reconditioned heels.
Some certain shapes of space
Conceal a greater death of freedom.

When we have lived and dreamed of doors
And counted out their opening
And closing,
Should we then jape on corridors
Of someone else's choosing?

Rhyming To Death

I met a man on Kilburn station

Said he planned to save the nation
Claimed he had a reputation
Far beyond the Iron Curtain
Then he said he was not certain
If he had the fare for Luton
Cried: Your help won't be forgotten
Wrote my name around the bottom
Of his escrivette.

I met a man on Kilburn station

Said he held the explanation
Good and Ill kiss in rotation
To achieve complete remission
Pay your debtors on the button
Then he asked the way to Horsham
Is it south or west of Sutton?
Wrote my name inside the carton
Of his Val de Loires.

I met a man on Kilburn station

With looks like mine
His hollow eyes were bitten bloodless
Rhyme by rhyme
I missed my train
And lost a partner for the second time

I walk to Brondesbury nowadays
And take the Richmond-Woolwich line.

(There was an Irish belief that children and cattle could be "eye bitten"
by an evil eye and then be "rhymed to death" by a witch)

Not To Die

They are trying not to die
On Villiers Street.
On John Adam Street
Beside the steps
That lead up to the Strand
They are living off glances
Loose gestures from smart handbag queens
And merchants of the quick dip.

On Hungerford Bridge
(The sixteenth favourite view of London)
There are two of them in place.
One at each end.
Folded up into the railings.
Squatting
To be down there
And not take up
Too much of the walking space.

Congruous
As eels on a tin plate.
They have curled themselves
Into our thumbs.
Yes – and we don't belong here.
Yes – but we're not gone yet.

Visits to Box Hill on Sundays
Will not cure us of this.
Watching the leaves turn brown

Feeling the structure of the earth.
This is another form of dying.
One that we balloted for
And cannot be rubbed out
By a tightening of the groin.

This is a different touch.
A gentle
Relentless stubbing of the big toe
Into the soft.

They are trying not to die on Villiers Street.
We disembowel ourselves
Rather too quietly.

The Goosey Night – A Lullaby

Mummy reads the small print
Daddy dims the light
Mummy dreams of windsails
With their wings washed white.

Daddy dreams of sandstorms
Baby cosselled high
Baby smiles and listens
For the long goosey night.

Mummy holds her body still
Daddy needs his sleep
Mummy dreams of winejars
With their rims stained deep.

Daddy dreams of courts of law
Baby's life untied
Baby hears and takes it
To the long goosey night.

Mummy wakes at keening time
Daddy leaves at eight
Mummy studied Descartes
And the Modern State.

Daddy trades comestibles
Baby's future bright
Baby heeds the empire
Of the long goosey night

Mummy hates the men of war
Daddy fears the priest
Daddy bought this bungalow
On a short lease.

Baby has a private view
Hope and faith denied
Baby has the knowing
Of the long goosey night

Fourth Station

Cricklewood station,
Cricklewood station.
I wait for the five o'clock
With indignation.
It's down to King's Cross
For a conversation
With a man in a bookshop
Creased with perspiration.

I've never seen the colours over west so hard,
Like ripples of blackcurrant on a faded postcard.
No coronas on the floodlights in the marshalling yard,
It's the kind of night God must have used
For passing on the word.

Graffiti on the shelters
On Cricklewood station,
Chalking the genetic code
Of mass imagination.
Putting out the candles
Of a deeper indignation.
Jumping on the five o'clock
For a private assignation.

I've never heard such singing of the voltage in the wire,
Like the suicidal pleadings of a tabernacle choir.
They can keep you out of work, they can't put out the fire.
It's the kind of night God must have used
To push sexual desire.

Graffiti say that God was here
On Cricklewood station.
If I had known it soon enough
I would have booked a conversation
To offer to that great divine
Heartfelt congratulation
For leaving us a night like this
In form of compensation.

I've never seen the moisture on the brick so sheer,
Like earrings that are clinging to a dead man's ear.
There's a cutting kind of silence in this section of the year.
It's the kind of night God must have used
To make his passion clear.

Cricklewood station,
Cricklewood station.
I wait for the five o'clock
With indignation.
It's down to King's Cross
For a brief flirtation
And the evening in the back row
Of a godless generation.

Never Really Knew Him

In Memory of PJ Fahy

After his funeral,
All that I saw were men with sticks.
On the edges of recognition, moving away.
A class of ghosts, ruddy faced, smiling.
A class of men if only I could tell.

Rain clattered on the pub windows.
Faces showed concern, but not too much.
"Was he a Galway man, or Clare?" they asked.
I shook my head, turned the drink away.

"I never really knew him" I said.
"Never really knew".
Remembering the way he bent at the office,
Took the microphone in the Hampden and sang.
"I never really knew him" I said.
Looked at the rain. Took up the offer.

Sometimes I notice his name.
Imagine his body at the foot of the steps.
Sometimes the memory of something opening.
A handshake, a shared table.
Sometimes a sense of something remaining.
Sometimes a poem in a half-filled hall.

At Camley Park, we met to mark his death.
Speeches, a song.
A small meeting, friends and unfamiliars.
Poetry, music, madness.
The same calling, the same cause.

Drugtime Cowboy Joe

Nutters get
Compulsory sunsets.
Wall to wall landscaping of the soul.
Always a rugged coast, salt-flecked but liveable.
Always a hero looking west,
Going on about the forward march of science.

You can have your sunsets cloudy bright,
Bright, bright to cloudy or extra bright
With cloudy intervals at intervals
And something special for that tickle
Of psychosis.

You can have them anyway you need.
But always numbing,
Perpetually numbing
And always, everlastingly,
Cold.

Nutters get
To stand at the window, drinking the sunset down,
Tasting no rain.
Feeling the cracks in their spirit
Silt up.

Nutters get compulsory sunsets.
Always start writing back:
Wish we weren't here.

Health Act

Hold me.
Hold me.
Hold me – cries the girl.
The girl in hospital clothes.
She kneels on tat carpet squares,
Knuckles the joins,
Rocks against the orange armchair,
Pressing her forehead into the texturene.
Hold me. Hold me – she cries
And turn that fucking television off.

The evening team are moving back out.
They have sat in the sluices,
Watching the clock pass eight.
Coolly they edge the room,
Reading their newspapers upside down.
Drift near the window curtains
Counting, counting, checking the back way out.
Hold me. Hold me.
Hold me. They gather round neatly,
Finger their cuffs in unison.

When will the slap come?
When will the blanket be brought?
Evans is Jesus.
Evans is the bastard.
Coming from the nursing station
With his blue suit on.
Every sympathy in order.

They take her to the treatment room,
They take her to seclusion.
Beyond harm's reach
And just in time to enter on the shift report.

At twenty past nine we'll make ourselves toast
And cluster in the servery.
We were the ones with the power to hold,
The power to make safe the danger.
We cannot act through want of health,
Angling for leave under Section Three,
Dreaming of mealtimes outside Saint David's.

We are the ones with the holding power.
Evans is our saver.
Evans is the bastard.

Night And Morning

The trains run down from Luton
Each hour throughout the night.
The clock of sanity lies winded on the floor.

Turn towards the thin partition,
Turn from the light.
The nurses' watch won't help you change this law.

The nurses read beside the passage door.
They read their stars and dream of nothing more.

The battered boys from Flanders
Rode this way from the docks.
They made them sweet and locked the passage door.

Turn towards the cold partition,
Turn away from their touch.
They've left those fields and joined a greater war.

Their names are scratched within the linen store.
The clothes you cadge are still the clothes they wore.

Men drove a railway eastwards.
One branch beyond the halt.
It curved within, beyond the workyard door.

Turn away from the cold partition,
Turn towards their touch.
You have to wake, you have to face the dawn.

The pigeons land and strut upon the lawn.
They peck the bread the nursing staff have thrown.

The morning trains speak differently,
Their thunder tuned by sight.
The clock has changed its digits and its tone.

Turn from the thin partition,
Turn towards the light.
The floors are bright, the floorboards still unclean.

You lose the night, your ancestors are known.
Only the clock and you are in the wrong.

*(First World War casualties were sent to Napsbury Asylum,
often disappearing into the mental health system)*

No Touching Point

She kneels in the corner with her face to the wall,
Her hands balled into fists, her dark hair
Falling across the shoulders.
Her back is slightly curved, her eyes are open.
You can just see the eyelashes moving.

You cannot reach her now, never knew
She had this in her when you dined at Cox's,
Rowed together on Derwent Water,
Stood in Penzance watching the ferry leave
For the Scillies. Her face sparkled with rain
Like any other. Her smile lit up the room.

Her skin is pale. A comforting arm might shatter
Her sanity.

How could you know that? How could you know
A natural movement might be so harmful?
Perhaps it is love, an unnatural knowledge.
Perhaps it is love. Perhaps you suspected it
All along.

Bring lavender. Soft light to tempt her out.
A cup of peppermint, some music, a steady eye
To watch over her.

How could you know that? How could you know
What to bring?
Perhaps it is love, a particular understanding.
Perhaps it is love. Perhaps you were touching her
All along.

Tomorrow, maybe she'll turn,
Accept a shawl, sit by the fire.
The clock will tick, the fire hiss.
Perhaps you will share a chair, talk a little.
Perhaps you will touch, a special communication.
Perhaps it is love. Perhaps you knew it
All along.

To Willie Emslie

You had that blown fuse look.
A straight ahead stare, hands hooked.
The extra pyramidals.
Out in the annexe, plugged in by the door,
You played with no flair Chuck Berry at our socials.

One guitar, one amp.
The annexe crammed.
Always Memphis, heavy on bass,
Drowning the thump of our suedes.
You always stood, after each turn,
Rubbing a hand over your smooth face.
Rocking, but not to the music.

Did you ride out the bad times, William?
Did you ever come back?
To rub the wee bit smiles into our gobs.
Did you get to be a farmer, running the grain
Through your big arms, yellow as yon jumper?
Did you ever play the Logierait Hotel on Saturdays
And make the women dance?

In London town I've done no better.
Maybe worse.
A home by a station, the sounds of travel
Fading from my ears. A few verses
Against the professionals.
An apt response, a burst of applause.
Some games in the park while the keepers
Were looking elsewhere.

We should have made the nurses jump
When we were young and decades were left.
I should have shouted for you not smiled against.
Because I was better, because their tests
Gave me more pinholes rather than less.

They cut us up alright, Willie.
And memory can only make the best of it.
Divided from each other, divided from ourselves.
No revolutions, no laughter in the losers' camp.
Only a hand rubbing across our faces
And Chuck Berry's Memphis played on one amp.

Hearing Impairment

He cannot hear doves.
Sound has lost its sweetness.
In church the music crumbles,
Curdling his senses.

His ears are filled with plastic,
A tube runs up to each rim.
He wears his hair long in all seasons,
Sits at the table with his back to the light.

Silence is a fair option,
Screening the loudness of strangers.
He can watch children whispering,
Read the words on their lips.

Rhythm has not gone,
He moves gracefully.
Coming down Church Street,
His fingers click.

This is not injury,
The beginning of a dark longing.
This is not terminal,
The end of true perception.

In Celandine's he laughs with the waitress,
Smells floor polish.
He watches the door-chimes, hears clatter from the kitchen.
Stands by an open window, feeling warmth in the air.

A Madman Teaching
(Clinical Psychology class – Autumn 2002)

A madman stands at the blackboard teaching.
He remembers the doctor had him there,
Pointing, questioning, silencing him
With his interpretations.

Bowing ever so slightly
At his audience.

A madman stands at the blackboard teaching.
He remembers the nurse putting the needle in,
Saying that it was all for his own good, that he wasn't
Quite right.

Bowing ever so slightly
Towards the chargehand.

A madman stands at the blackboard teaching.
He remembers that the ward is closed,
The asylum shuttered.

A madman stands at the blackboard teaching.
This is our day.
This is our century.

Coming Out

A cold winter morning on Acacia Ward.
There's the sound of something stirring
And it isn't the birds.
There's the sound of someone singing.
An event has occurred.
A sleeping giant is waking
And it means to be heard.

That we're coming out. We are coming out.
And we're coming out all right.
That we're coming out and we're coming out
And we're coming out for our rights.

We never asked for special status.
To be one sign of God's dismay.
We never asked for the asylums but they built them
Anyway.
As the pundits all pontificate about community decay,
We're just popping in your front door
With something to say.

That we're coming out. We are coming out.
And we're coming out all right.
That we're staying out. That we're stopping out
And we're stopping out for our rights.

They don't want us on the pavements.
They don't want us in the bus.
They claim that we're non-civil,
That we're just too strange to trust.

Well, we wish to stay unbiased,
We don't want to make a fuss.
But we've taken down a wee vote here
And it's quite unanimous.

That we're coming out. WE ARE COMING OUT.
And we're coming out all right.
We are staying out. We are stopping out
And we're stopping out
For our rights.

In Your Warm Arms

In your warm arms
The day came in less like a vagrant
Selling tins,
Less like a loon with a milky skin.
In your warm arms the day came in
Whispering.

At your neck
The day could seem
Less like a tinker's twisted schemes,
Less like a harvest standing green.
In your dark eyes
The world could seem
Welcoming.

The toss of a cold city.
Handsome strangers.
Encountering the gap between ideals
And the steamless beat of logic.
Arguing, winnowing,
Waiting
For the sound of your feet.

In your warm arms
The night came in less like a hawker
Overspent,
Less like a gambler's discontent.
In your warm arms the night came in
Whispering.

The Pain Of Love

The pain of love is terrible.
Coasters slip in unseen
Before the hoot of dawn.
They weigh against the knuckled piers.
Oily water lisps at their sides
And seagulls eat the scraps.
The pain of love bites like an early squall.

The pleasure of love is terrible.
We untie the world.
Bookham, Egham and Dorking fields –
They are listed with Barbary.
Poppies snag the nearest corn,
The rooks wheel down.
The pleasure of love bites like harvest mice.

The pain of love is terrible.
Why should he die and be lost to my touch?
Only in agony now do I watch him.
Only the deathless tie,
Linking us between the eyes.
Only that heart which cannot stop
Nor can ever be made to.
The pain of love bites like a benison.